All Rights Reserved 2017 by Taylor Made Publishing, LLC©

No part of this book may be reproduced or transmitted in any form or by any means, graphics, electronic, or mechanical, including photocopying, recording, taping, or by any information storage retrieval system, without the permission in writing from the publisher.

Taylor Made Publishing, LLC
PO Box 861 Greenville, NC 27835
www.taylormadebooks.com

copyright #
ISBN: 978-0-9965937-7-9
Editor: Jorge L. Hernandez
Printed in USA.

DEDICATION

I DEDICATE THIS BOOK TO MY BEAUTIFUL CHILDREN, MORGAN AND GARRETT AND MY AMAZING NIECES AND NEPHEWS.

I WANT EACH OF YOU TO LOVE ALL OF WHAT MAKES YOU UNIQUE!
FROM YOUR MAGNIFICENT MINDS TO YOUR SENSATIONAL SHADES AND HUES.

I ALSO DEDICATE THIS BOOK TO ALL THE AMAZING CHILDREN REPRESENTING THE INCREDIBLE DIVERSITY OF HUMANITY. DON'T LET ANYONE PREVENT YOU FROM LOVING THE AMAZING
SKIN YOU'RE IN!

G. TODD TAYLOR

Today's the big day.
It was time for the big move.
Liz and Mac were so excited they didn't know what to do.

They were starting a new school.
Dad had a new job, bought a new house by the park.
It was time for a new adventure; it was time for a new start.

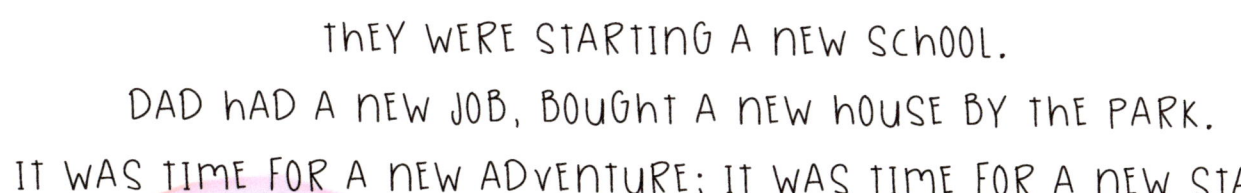

LIZ PUT ON HER PINK SHIRT WITH HER POLKA-DOT PANTS
AND RAN DOWN STAIRS JUST AS FAST AS SHE CAN.
MAC WAS SITTING AT THE TABLE WAITING IN STYLE
WITH HIS RED SHOES, YELLOW SHIRT AND A GREAT BIG SMILE.

MOM WAS THERE STANDING WITH A CURIOUS SMIRK,
AND DAD BLEW KISSES AS HE RAN OFF TO WORK.

THE KIDS LOOKED EXCITED; MOM'S SMIRK GREW TO A CHUCKLE.
SHE SAID "I LOVE YOUR BRIGHT COLORS. MAC, I LOVE YOUR BELT BUCKLE.
TODAY IS GOING TO BE GREAT. YOU KIDS ARE GOING TO MAKE A SPLASH.
NOW HURRY ALONG, I DON'T WANT YOU TO BE LATE FOR CLASS."
THE KIDS STUFFED THEIR FACES WITH EGGS, TOAST AND BERRIES,
THEN RAN TO CATCH THE BUS..."RUN, RUN, HURRY!"

AS THEY TOOK THEIR SEATS THINGS LOOKED A BIT STRANGE.
ALL OF THE KIDS LOOKED EXACTLY THE SAME!
THEY WORE THE SAME CLOTHES FROM THEIR SHIRTS TO THEIR SHOES.
THEY WORE THE SAME COLORS, SAME SHADE, SAME HUES.

Their hair was the same,
they even sat the same way.
Mac and Liz were astonished;
they didn't know what to say.

No one spoke, or even noticed they were there.
Liz and Mac just held hands
and slumped down in their chair.

THE BUS PULLED UP TO THE SCHOOL AND STOPPED WITH A SQUEAL.
THE KIDS LOOKED AT THE SCHOOL, IT DIDN'T LOOK REAL.

The whole place was blank, from the roof to the door.
When they walked inside, it even had white floors.

The teachers looked alike and spoke the same way.
No "hello", or "what's up," all they said was "Good day."
Liz and Mac were nervous. This school was like no other.
They've never been to a place that had absolutely no color!

She sent them out at once to Mr. Changamagoo.
He said, "Hello, how can I help you?"
He looked at their clothes and knew at once what to do.

HE CHANGED THEIR BRIGHT CLOTHES,
THEIR BOWS AND SHOES.
THEY HAD NO MORE COLOR,
NO SHADES OR HUES.
THEY WERE JUST LIKE EVERYONE ELSE,
NO LONGER FREE
TO JUST BE THEMSELVES,
WHO THEY WERE MEANT TO BE.

NOW LIZ AND MAC LOOKED
JUST LIKE ONE ANOTHER.
MR. CHANGAMAGOO HAPPILY SAID,
"NOW I DON'T SEE COLOR!"

They went back to class, their hearts in their socks.
Their hearts felt heavy, like a bag of rocks.
"I don't like this place Mac," Liz said with a whine.

"Why don't they see color? I happen to love mine."

Mac looked at his sister, a tear ran down her cheek.
He could take no more, he sprang from his seat.

"MS MARY!" MAC SAID AS HE MUSTERED UP STRENGTH.
"I'VE HAD ENOUGH, MY PATIENCE HAS REACHED ITS LENGTH!
WHY CAN'T YOU SEE COLOR, OR SHADES OR HUES?
WHY CAN'T YOU SEE GREENS OR PURPLES, OR REDS OR BLUES?!
WHY DON'T YOU SEE THE BRIGHT CLOTHES I WEAR. WHY CAN'T I BE FREE
TO BE WHO I AM, WHO I WAS MEANT TO BE?!"

The elephant was the one that wanted everyone just alike. He was the one that removed the color from their sight. He hated color and hues were not right.

He wanted all people to look just alike. The elephant scowled at the sister and the brother. "I want everyone to be equal, so I don't see color!!"

LIZ LOOKED AT MAC, THEY KNEW WHAT TO DO.
IF THEY EVER WANTED TO BE HAPPY, THE ELEPHANT MUST SHOO!
LIZ LOOKED THE BIG ELEPHANT SQUARE IN HIS TRUNK.
AND TOLD THAT ELEPHANT EXACTLY WHAT SHE THUNK.

"MR ELEPHANT," SHE SAID, "WE WANT OUR COLORS BACK RIGHT AWAY.
WE DON'T WANT TO LIVE LIKE THIS ONE MORE DAY!"
THE OTHER KIDS WERE SCARED, BUT THEN BEGAN TO CHEER.
THEN MAC GRABBED THE ELEPHANT BY HIS BIG ELEPHANT EAR.

"MR ELEPHANT," HE SAID, "ITS TIME FOR YOU TO GO.
WE DON'T WANT TO LIVE LIKE THIS ANYMORE!"
ALL THE KIDS PUSHED AND SHOVED THE ELEPHANT AWAY.
"SIT DOWN BE QUIET!", MS. MARY BEGAN TO SAY.

Ms. Mary was angry, she gasped and swooned.
She couldn't believe these kids kicked the elephant out of the room!
"I can't believe you did that! Are you kids insane?
Don't you know the world is better when we are all the same?
I don't see color, that's the best way to be.
If I don't see color, then everyone is just like me!"

But the kids kept pushing and with one final whack, the elephant was gone and he wasn't coming back!

And as if by magic a rainbow appeared, and Ms. Mary saw colors she hadn't seen in years.

She saw all the reds, the purples and blues. She saw all the colors, the shades and the hues.

Liz was excited, her polka dots came back. She had all her colors, and so did Mac!

Liz had her bows. Mac had his belt buckle.

They were both so excited all they could do was chuckle.

They were all so beautiful, in their own special way.
"I see your color!" they heard Ms. Mary say.
"I see your reds, your purples, your blues.
I see your colors, your shades, your hues.
There's no need to take your colors away.
I can appreciate your color, your hue and your shade."

MAC AND LIZ HAD ALL THEIR COLOR, SHADES AND HUES.
SO DID ALL THE TEACHERS AND THE STUDENTS, TOO.
MS. MARY FINALLY SAW COLOR, AND NOT A MOMENT TOO SOON.
ALL BECAUSE THEY FINALLY DEALT WITH THE ELEPHANT IN THE ROOM.

About the Author

Author G. Todd Taylor has been committed to uplifting the lives of youth for over 20 years. At an early age, he recognized the issues facing his community and has since worked diligently to solve them. His works are geared towards highlighting positive parenting and assisting youth in developing strong resiliencies to promote healthy lifestyles. Over the years, he was worked as school teacher, a counselor, an entrepreneur and a community activist. Of all the titles he has possessed, the title of Dad is the one he cherishes most.

Be sure to check out his other books, 'Dad Who Will I Be', and 'Daddy's Little Princess' available at GToddTaylor.com.

Printed in the USA
CPSIA information can be obtained
at www.ICGtesting.com
LVHW062134041023

760188LV00026B/94